This workbook bel

MW01012987

Hello 你好 nǐ hǎo

This workbook is for practicing to write Chinese characters. Pinyin, English translations and pictures are used to describe the characters. Write two pages at least two times a week. Think about the pronounciation, meaning and stroke order of each character while writing.

Trace over the gray characters by following the correct numbered stroke order as shown for the first few grids. Do not worry about the thickness of the gray lines. Use a pencil or pen to trace down the middle of the gray lines. Practice with the 2 sample grids below.

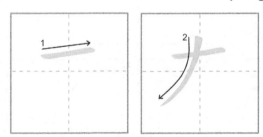

Thank you for choosing **Chinese For Kids First 50 Characters Ages 5+ (Simplified)**. Have fun writing and learning!

Chinese For Kids First 50 Characters Ages 5+ (Simplified)

ISBN-13: 978-1717386250
ISBN-10: 1717386253

© 2018 Queenie Law
Adore Neko Designs (www.adoreneko.com)

yī
one

Color the stroke for 一 (one).

1

1 stroke

🐟 Trace and write the Chinese character 一 (one).

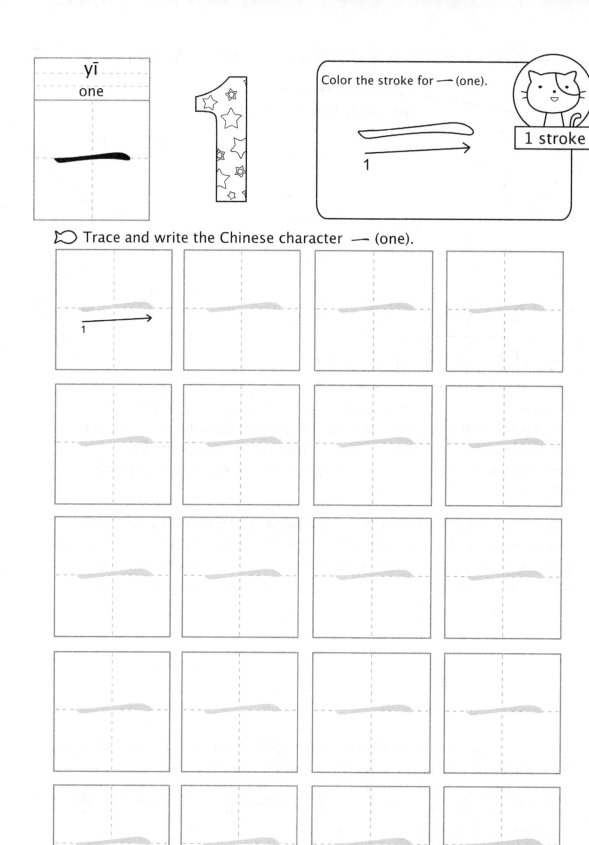

1

2

Help the fish 鱼 find the cat 猫. Trace the 一 from the fish 鱼 to the cat 猫.

Trace and write the Chinese character 一.

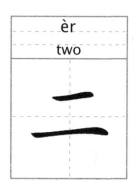

èr

two

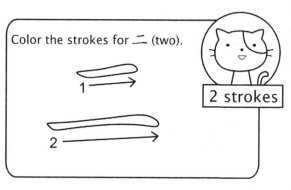

Color the strokes for 二 (two).

1 →

2 →

2 strokes

Trace and write the Chinese character 二 (two).

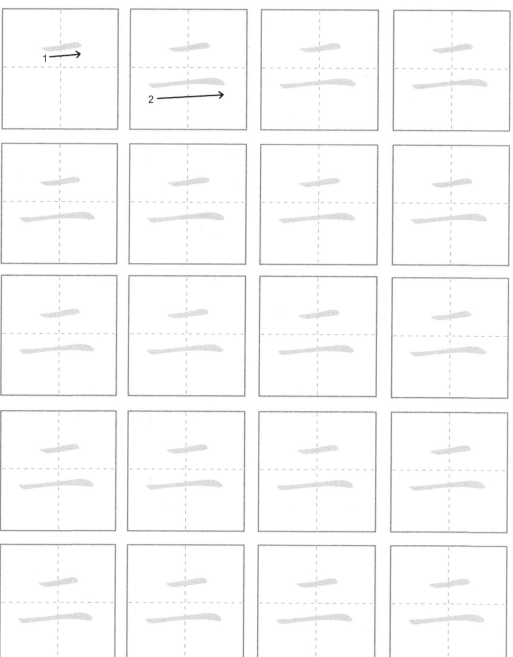

Trace the character 二 from the fish 鱼 to the cat 猫.

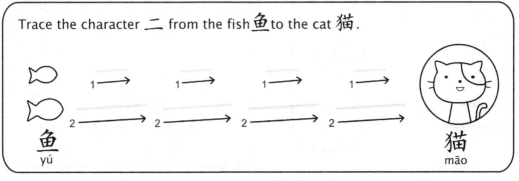

鱼
yú

猫
māo

Trace and write the Chinese character 二.

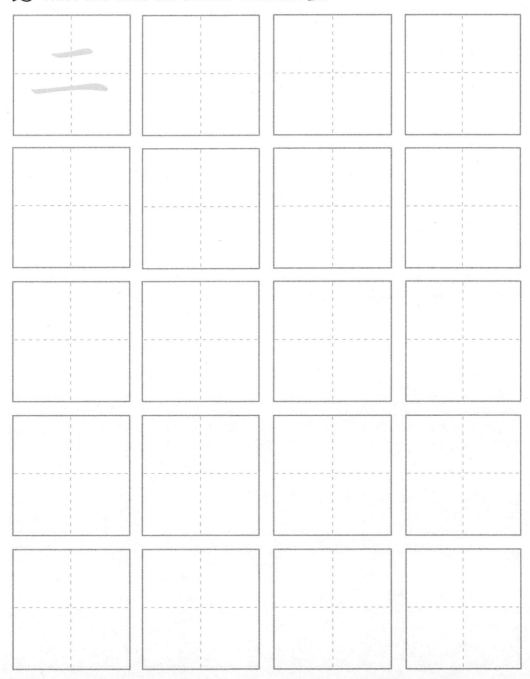

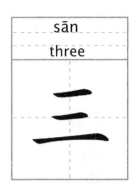

sān

three

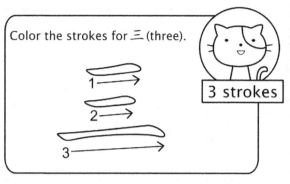

Color the strokes for 三 (three).

1 ⟶
2 ⟶
3 ⟶

3 strokes

🐟 Trace and write the Chinese character 三 (three).

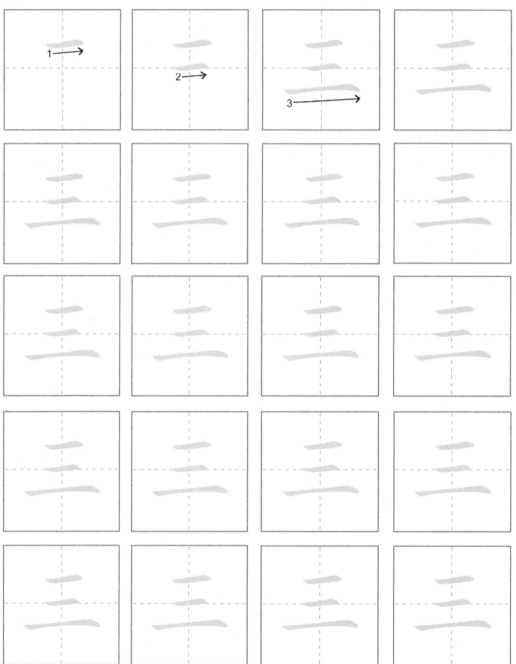

Trace the character 三 from the fish 鱼 to the cat 猫.

鱼
yú

猫
māo

Trace and write the Chinese character 三 .

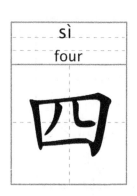

sì

four

四

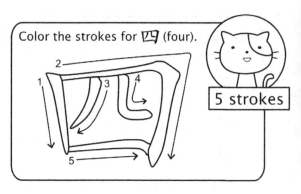

Color the strokes for 四 (four).

5 strokes

🐟 Trace and write the Chinese character 四 (four).

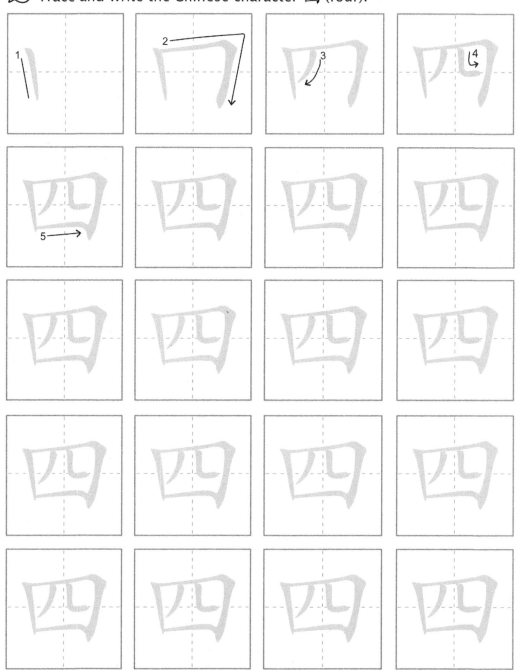

8

Starting from the cat 猫. Write the missing stroke for 四 in each fish 鱼.

猫
māo

鱼
yú

四 四 四 四 四

Trace and write the Chinese character 四.

wǔ
five

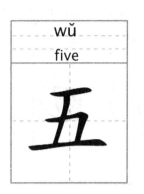

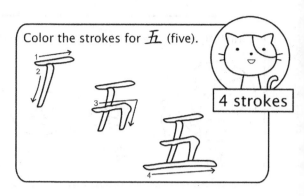

Trace and write the Chinese character 五 (five).

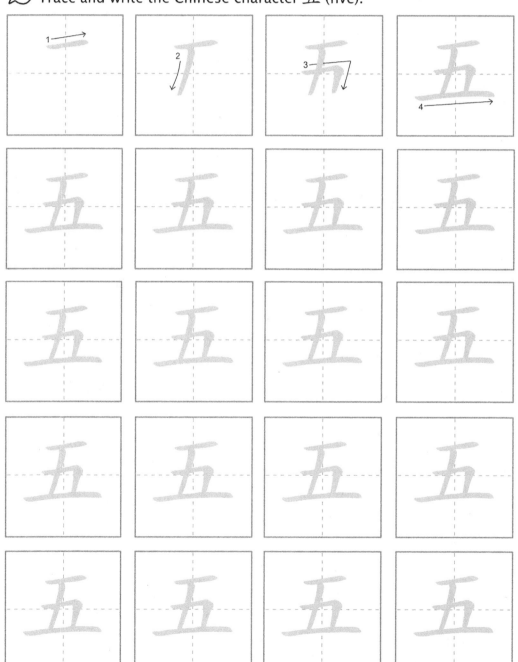

Write the missing stroke for 五 in each bubble from the fish 鱼 to the cat 猫.

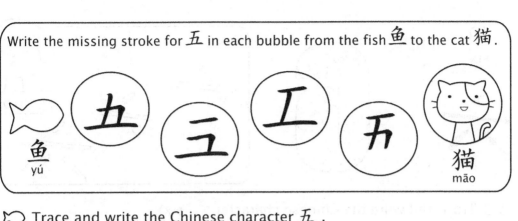

🐟 Trace and write the Chinese character 五 .

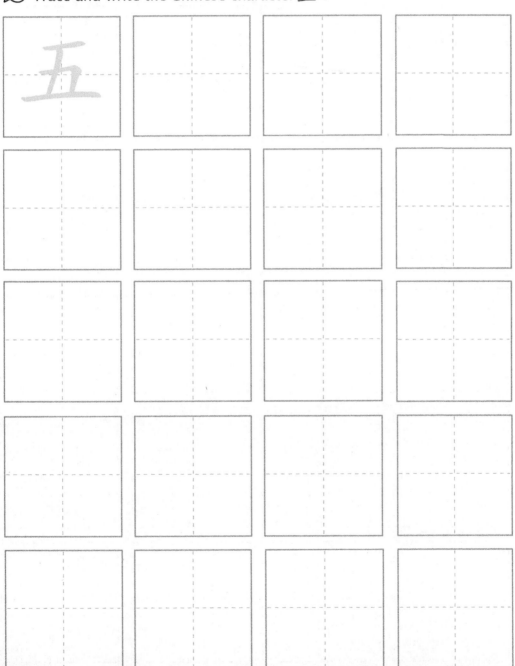

liù
six

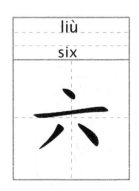

Color the strokes for 六 (six).

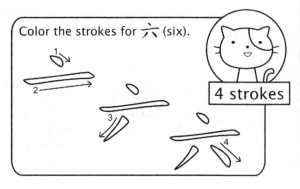

4 strokes

Trace and write the Chinese character 六 (six).

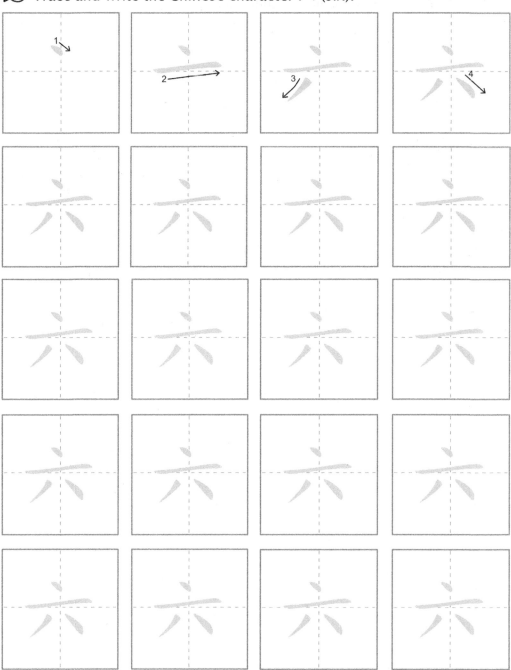

12

Write the missing stroke for 六 in each bubble from the fish 鱼 to the cat 猫.

鱼
yú

六   八   六   宀

猫
māo

Trace and write the Chinese character 六.

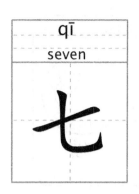

qī

seven

七

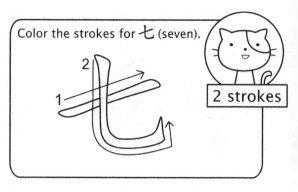

Color the strokes for 七 (seven).

2 strokes

Trace and write the Chinese character 七 (seven).

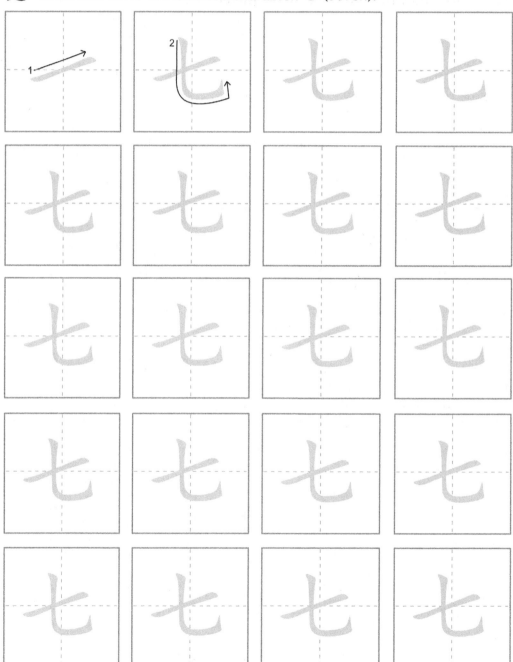

Write the missing stroke for 七 on the waves from the cat 猫 to the fish 鱼.

猫
māo

乚

一

乚   一

鱼
yú

Trace and write the Chinese character 七 .

七

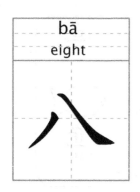

bā
eight

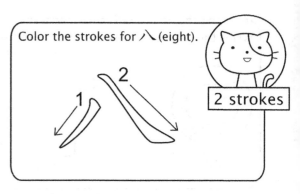

Color the strokes for 八 (eight).

2 strokes

🐟 Trace and write the Chinese character 八 (eight).

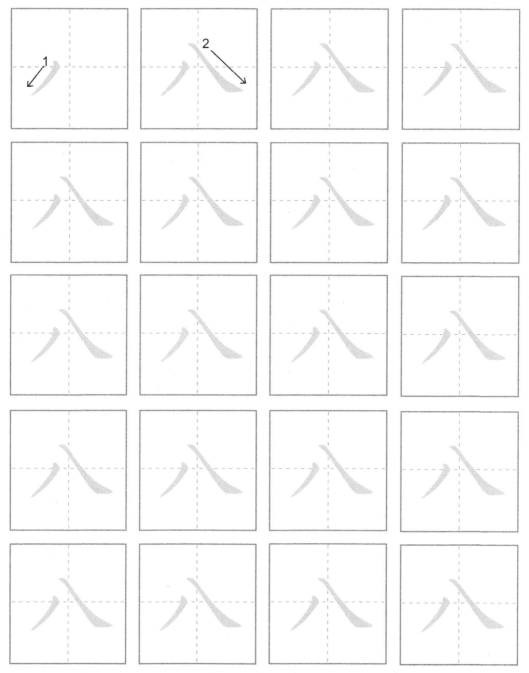

Write the missing stroke for 八 on the waves from the cat 猫 to the fish 鱼.

猫
māo

鱼
yú

Trace and write the Chinese character 八.

| jiǔ |
| nine |

九

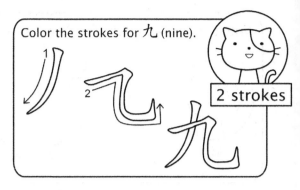

🐟 Trace and write the Chinese character 九 (nine).

Write the missing stroke for 九 on the waves from the cat 猫 to the fish 鱼.

乙

乙 ノ

ノ

猫
māo

鱼
yú

Trace and write the Chinese character 九 .

九

shí
ten

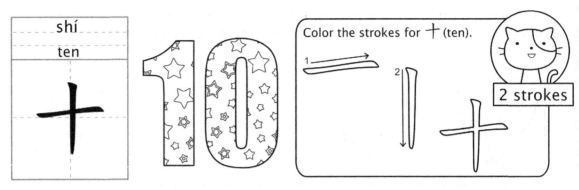

Color the strokes for 十 (ten).

2 strokes

🐟 Trace and write the Chinese character 十 (ten).

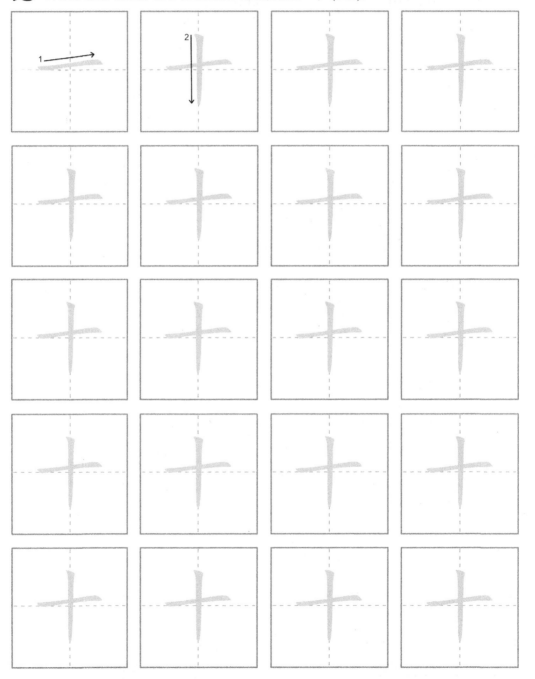

Write the missing stroke for 十 on the waves from the cat 猫 to the fish 鱼.

猫
māo

鱼
yú

Trace and write the Chinese character 十 .

Good Job!

Practice writing characters you have learned below.

Name

Date

Good Job!

Practice writing characters you have learned below.

23

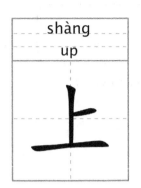

shàng

up

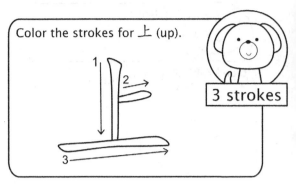
Trace and write the Chinese character 上 (up).

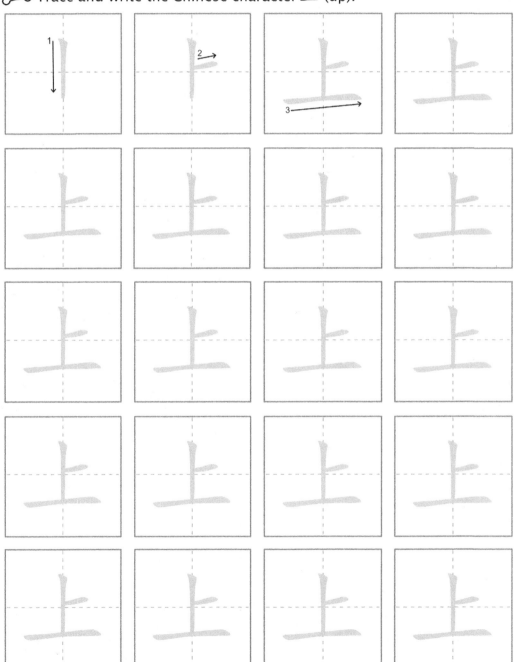

Write the missing stroke for 上 on each button from the dog 狗 to the bone 骨.

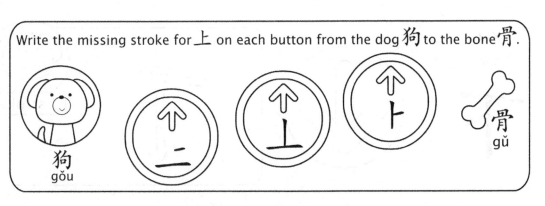

Trace and write the Chinese character 上 .

xià
down

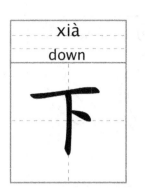

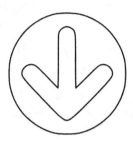

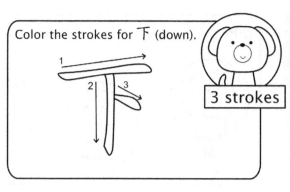

3 strokes

Trace and write the Chinese character 下 (down).

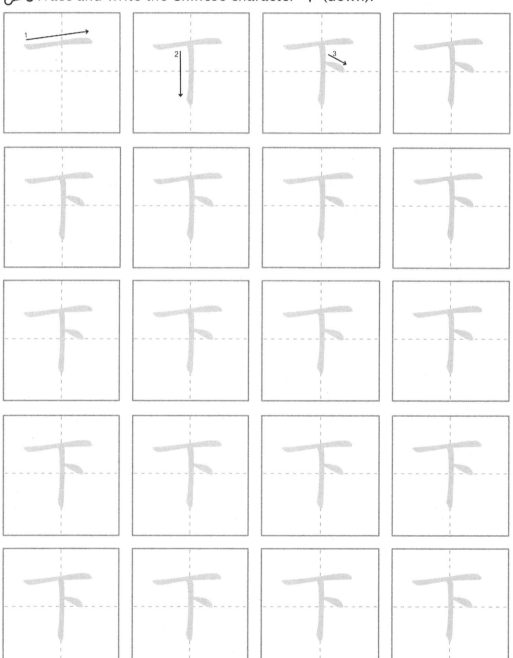

26

Write the missing stroke for 下 on each button from the dog 狗 to the bone 骨.

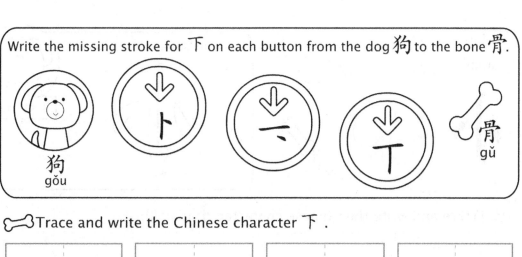

Trace and write the Chinese character 下 .

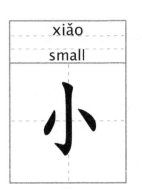

xiǎo

small

小

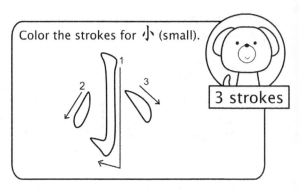
Trace and write the Chinese character 小 (small).

Write the missing stroke for 小 on each bowl from the dog 狗 to the bone 骨.

狗
gǒu

八

小

小

骨
gǔ

Trace and write the Chinese character 小 .

dà
big

大

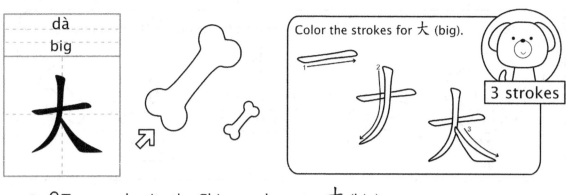

Color the strokes for 大 (big).

3 strokes

Trace and write the Chinese character 大 (big).

Write the missing stroke for 大 on each bowl from the dog 狗 to the bone 骨.

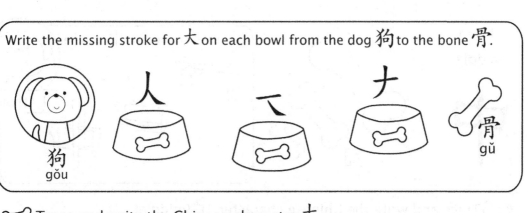

狗 gǒu

人

乀

ナ

骨 gǔ

Trace and write the Chinese character 大 .

zhōng
middle
中

Color the strokes for 中 (middle).

4 strokes

Trace and write the Chinese character 中 (middle).

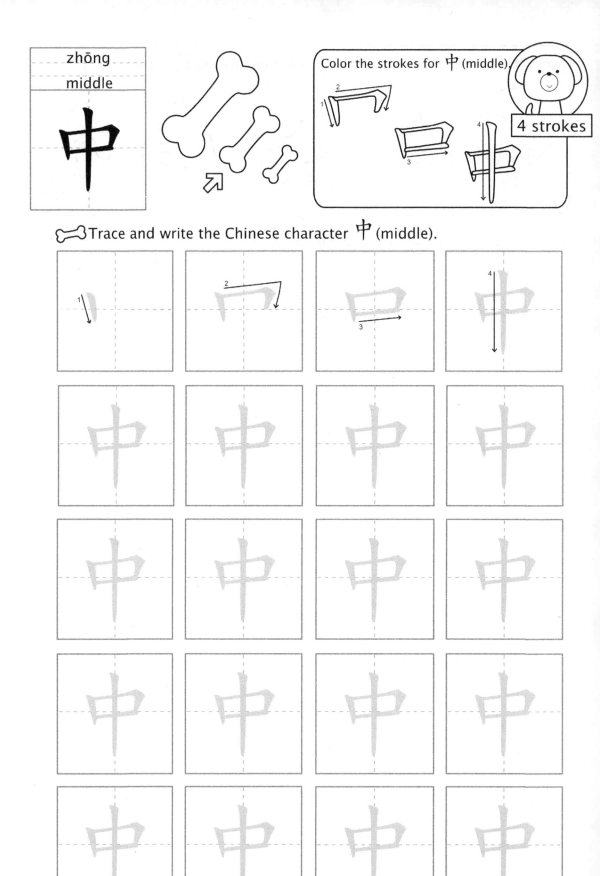

Write the missing stroke for 中 on each bowl from the dog 狗 to the bone 骨.

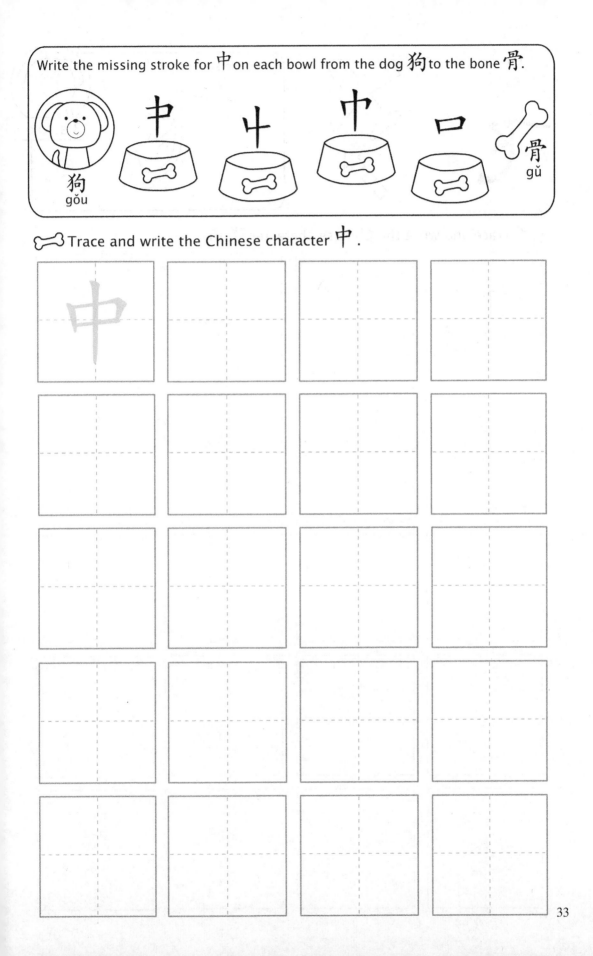

狗
gǒu

骨
gǔ

Trace and write the Chinese character 中 .

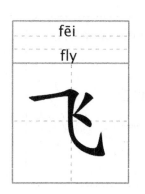

fēi

fly

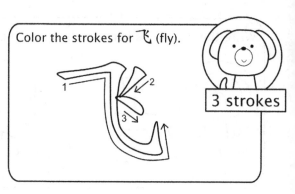
🦴 Trace and write the Chinese character 飞 (fly).

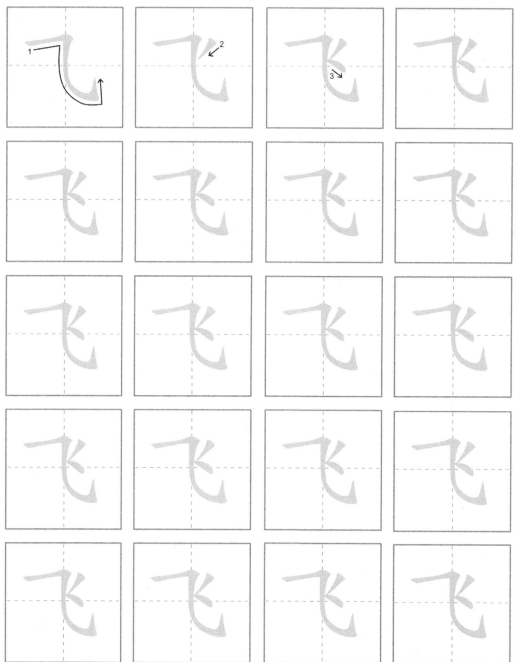

Write the missing stroke for 飞 on each bowl from the dog 狗 to the bone 骨.

狗
gǒu

骨
gǔ

Trace and write the Chinese character 飞 .

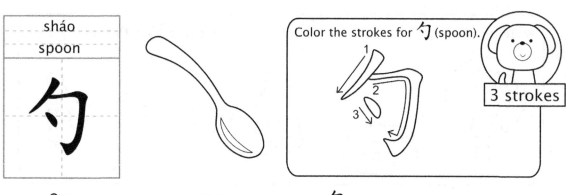

sháo
spoon
勺

Color the strokes for 勺 (spoon).

3 strokes

🦴 Trace and write the Chinese character 勺 (spoon).

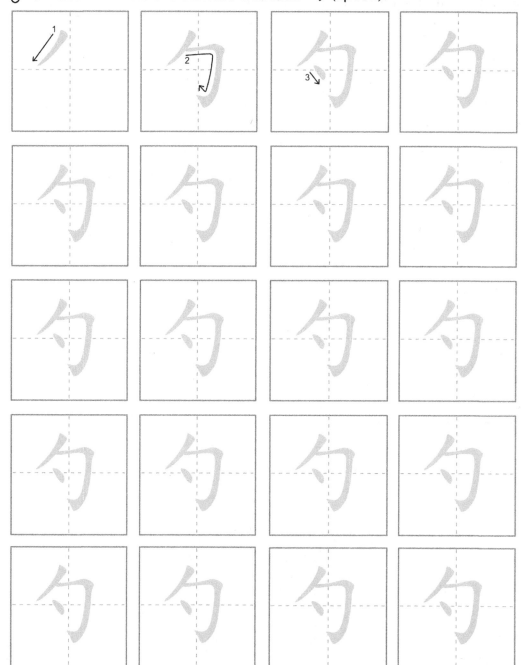

Write the missing stroke for 勺 on each bowl from the dog 狗 to the bone 骨.

狗
gǒu

骨
gǔ

Trace and write the Chinese character 勺 .

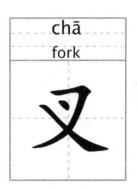

chā

fork

叉

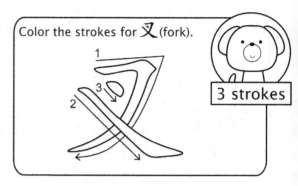

Color the strokes for 叉 (fork).

3 strokes

🦴 Trace and write the Chinese character 叉 (fork).

Write the missing stroke for 叉 on each fork from the dog 狗 to the bone 骨.

狗
gǒu

ヽ

フ

又

骨
gǔ

Trace and write the Chinese character 叉.

叉

míng
name

名

HELLO
my name is

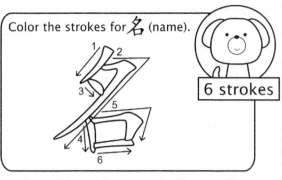
Trace and write the Chinese character 名 (name).

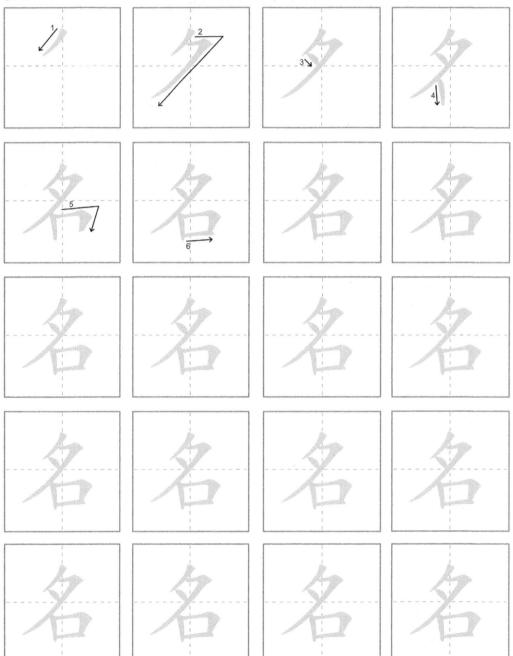

Write the missing stroke for 名 on each name card from the dog 狗 to the bone 骨.

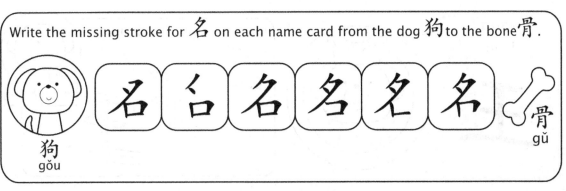

狗
gǒu

骨
gǔ

Trace and write the Chinese character 名.

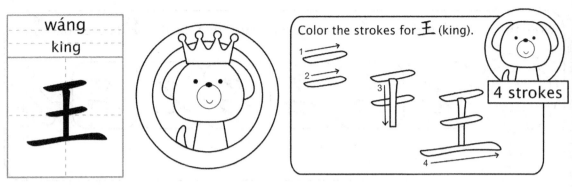

wáng
king

王

Color the strokes for 王 (king).

4 strokes

🦴 Trace and write the Chinese character 王 (king).

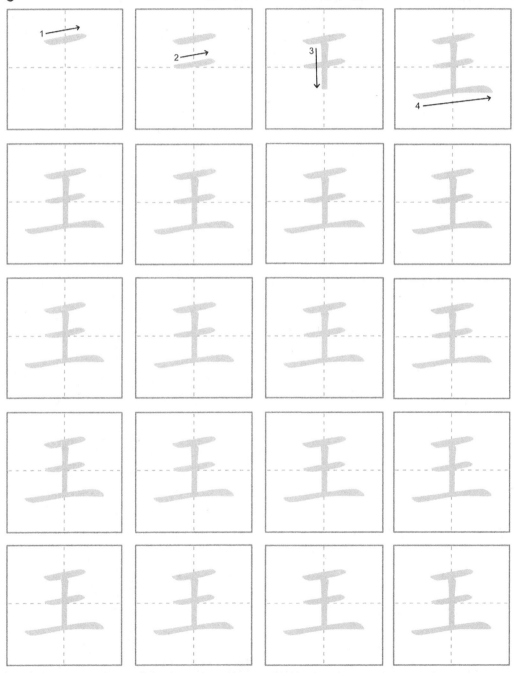

Write the missing stroke for 王 on each crown from the dog 狗 to the bone 骨.

🦴 Trace and write the Chinese character 王.

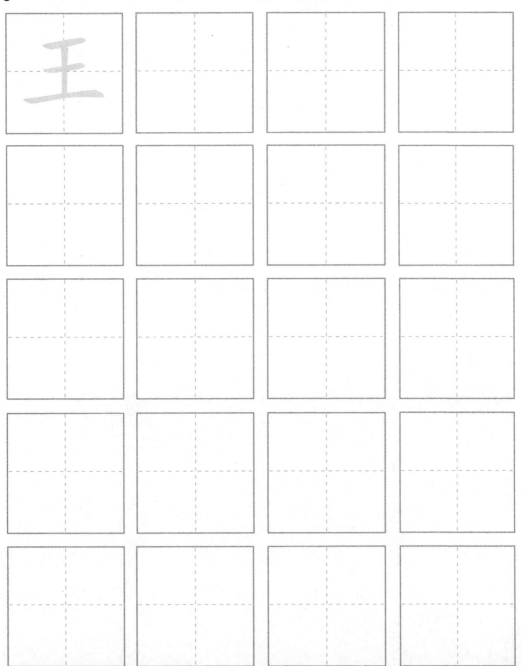

Good Job! Practice writing characters you have learned below.

Good Job! Practice writing characters you have learned below.

rì
sun

日

Color the strokes for 日 (sun).

4 strokes

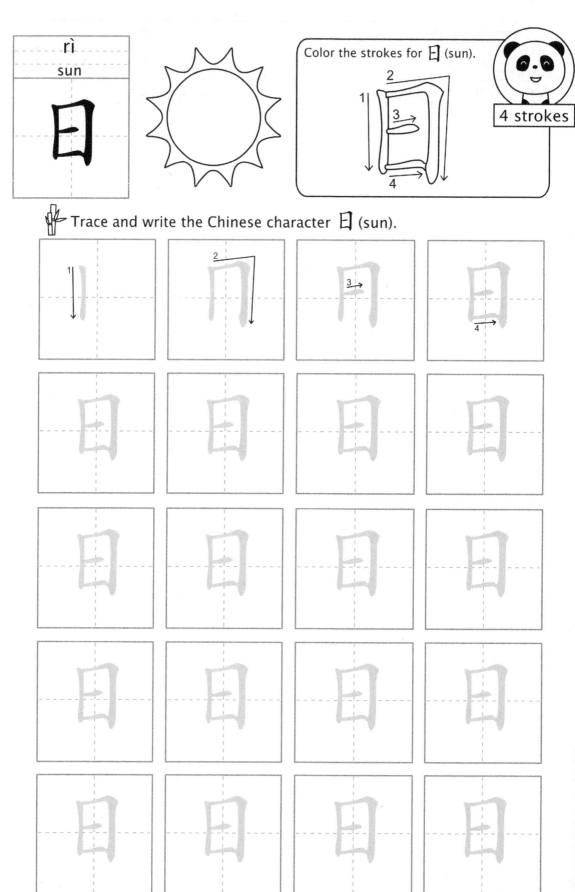

Trace and write the Chinese character 日 (sun).

46

Write the missing stroke for 日 on each sun from the panda 熊猫 to the bamboo 竹子.

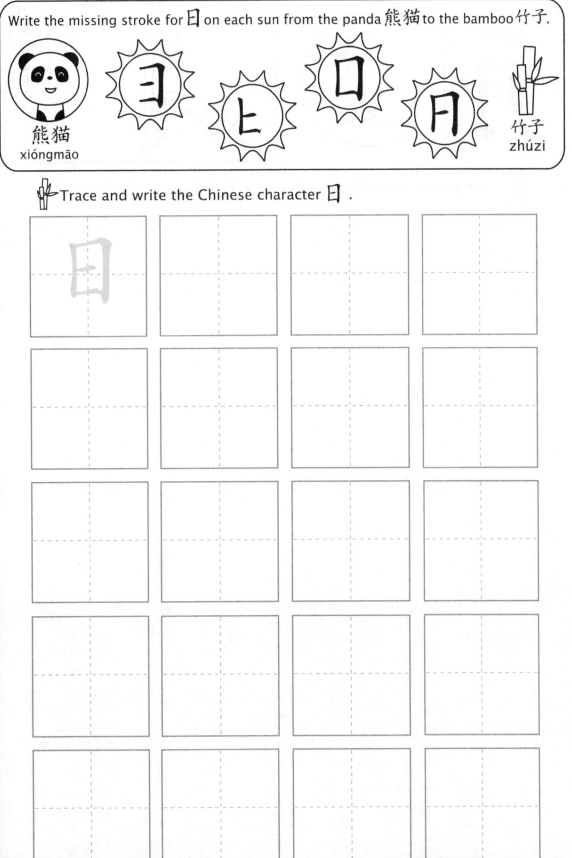

熊猫
xióngmāo

竹子
zhúzi

Trace and write the Chinese character 日 .

yuè
moon

月

Color the strokes for 月 (moon).

4 strokes

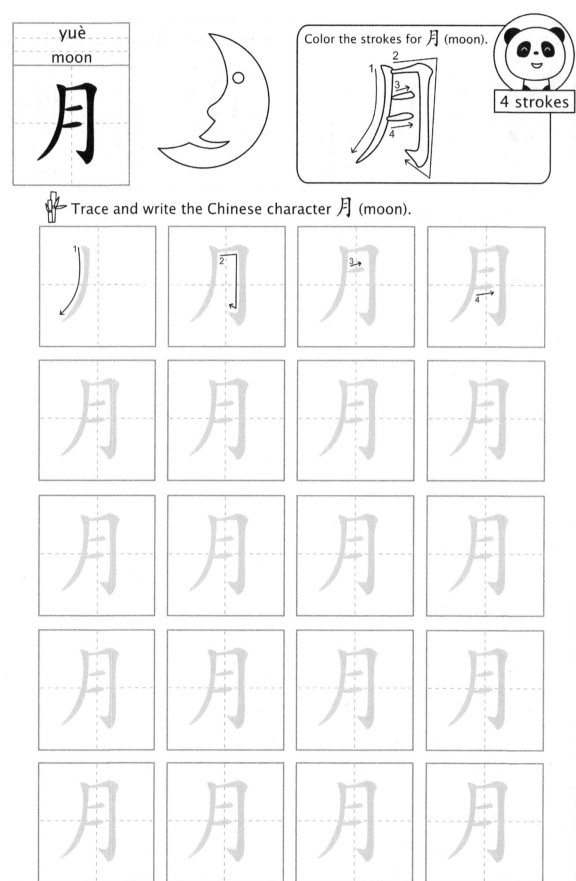

Trace and write the Chinese character 月 (moon).

Write the missing stroke for 月 on each moon from the panda 熊猫 to the bamboo 竹子.

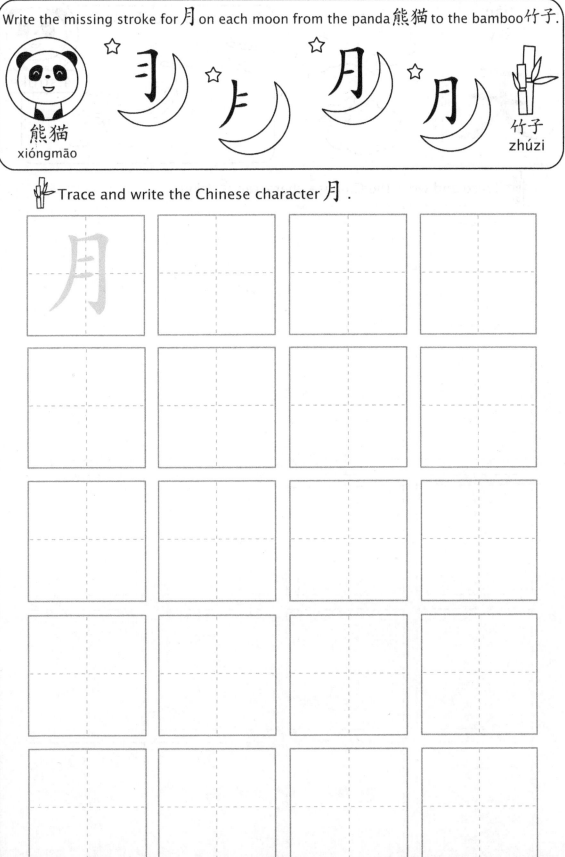

熊猫
xióngmāo

竹子
zhúzi

Trace and write the Chinese character 月 .

| tiān |
| sky |

天

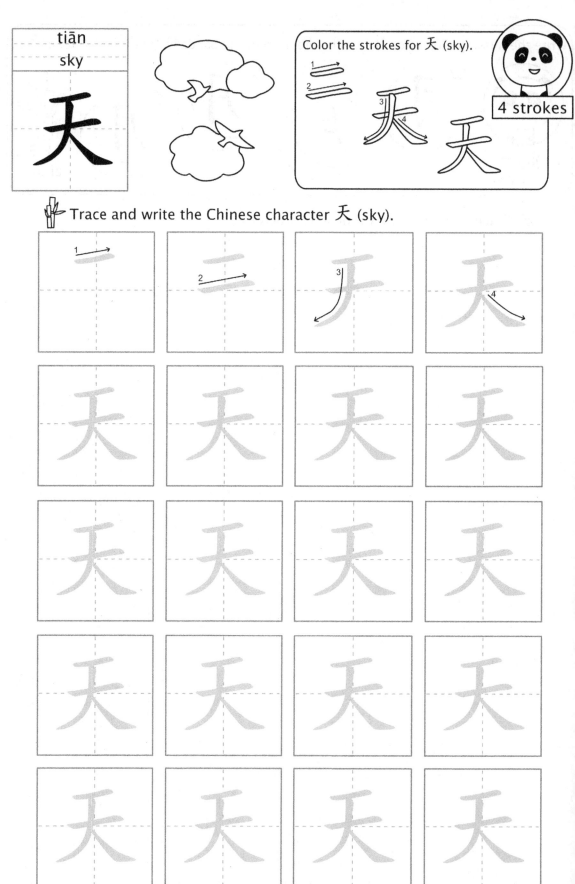

Color the strokes for 天 (sky).

4 strokes

Trace and write the Chinese character 天 (sky).

50

Write the missing stroke for 天 in the sky from the panda熊猫 to the bamboo竹子.

熊猫
xióngmāo

大

人

二

王

竹子
zhúzi

Trace and write the Chinese character 天 .

天

yǔ
rain

雨

8 strokes

Trace and write the Chinese character 雨 (rain).

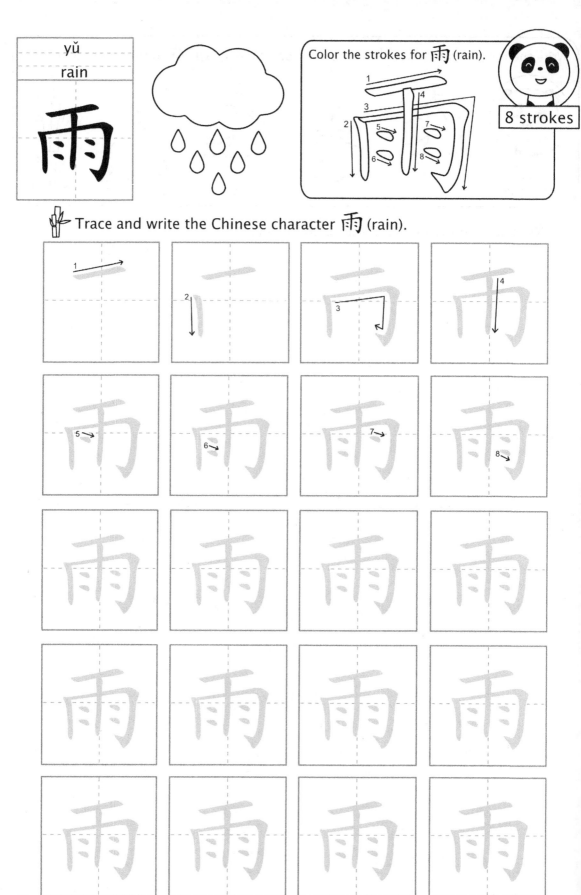

Write the missing strokes for 雨 in each raindrop from the panda 熊猫 to the bamboo 竹子.

熊猫
xióngmāo

竹子
zhúzi

Trace and write the Chinese character 雨.

yún

cloud

云

Color the strokes for 云 (cloud).

1
2
3
4

4 strokes

Trace and write the Chinese character 云 (cloud).

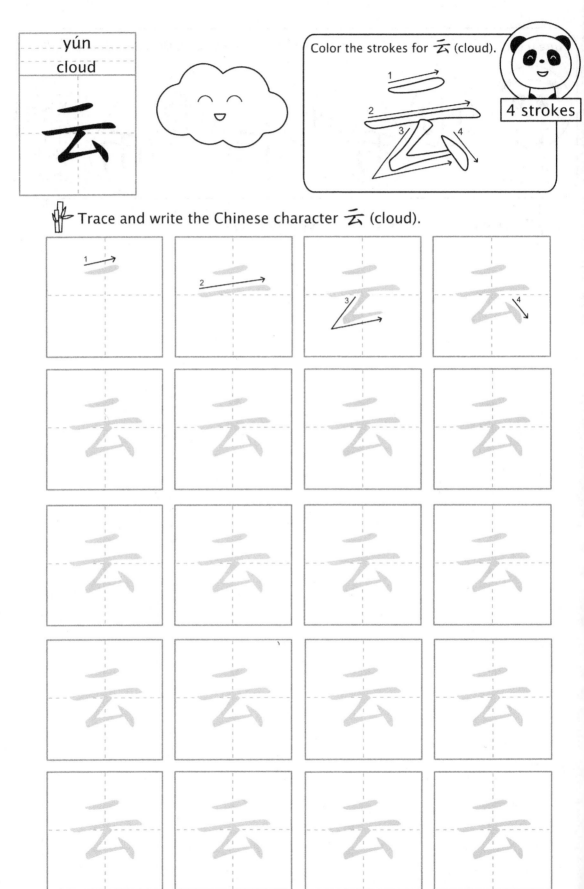

Write the missing stroke for 云 in each cloud from the panda 熊猫 to the bamboo 竹子.

熊猫
xióngmāo

云　云　云　云

竹子
zhúzi

 Trace and write the Chinese character 云 .

bèi
shell

贝

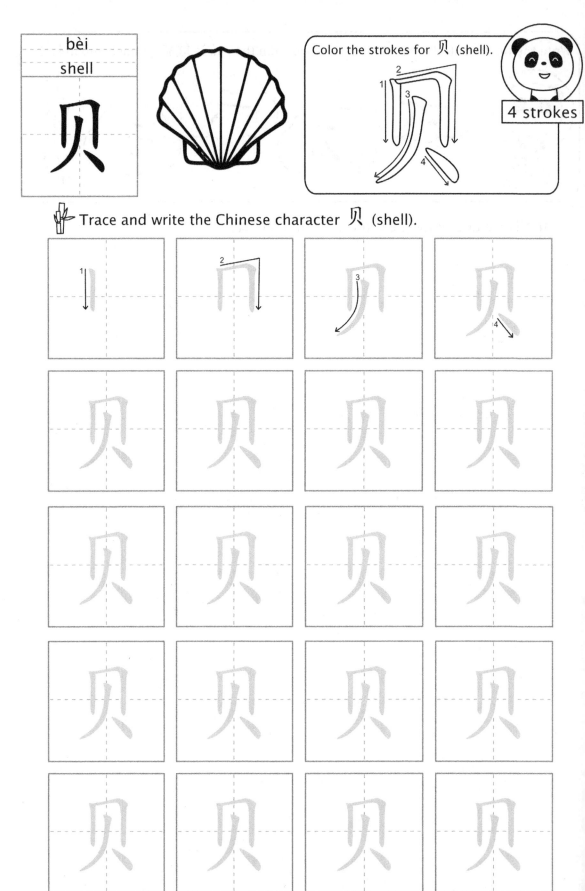

Trace and write the Chinese character 贝 (shell).

Write the missing stroke for 贝 in each shell from the panda 熊猫 to the bamboo 竹子.

熊猫
xióngmāo

竹子
zhúzi

Trace and write the Chinese character 贝 .

yú

fish

鱼

Color the strokes for 鱼 (fish).

8 strokes

Trace and write the Chinese character 鱼 (fish).

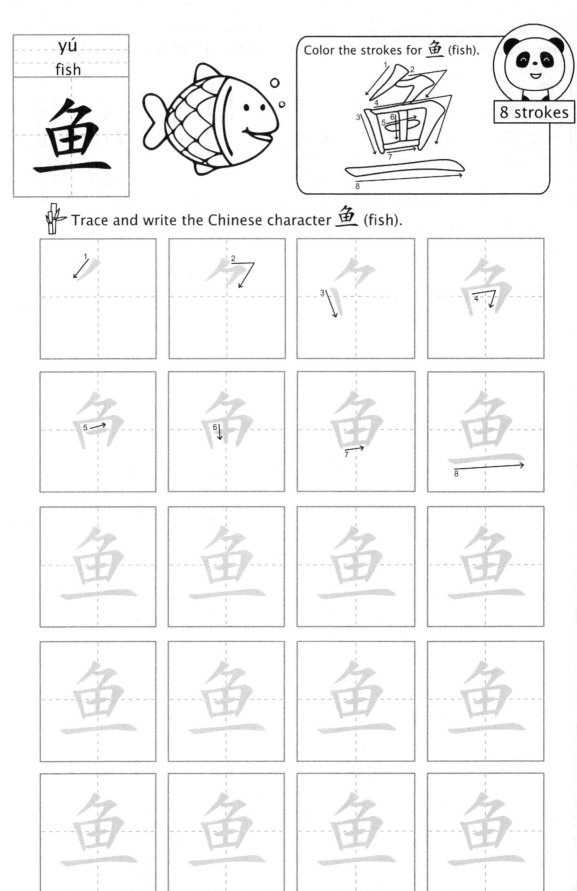

Write the missing strokes for 鱼 in each fish from the panda 熊猫 to the bamboo 竹子.

熊猫
xióngmāo

竹子
zhúzi

Trace and write the Chinese character 鱼.

chóng
worm

虫

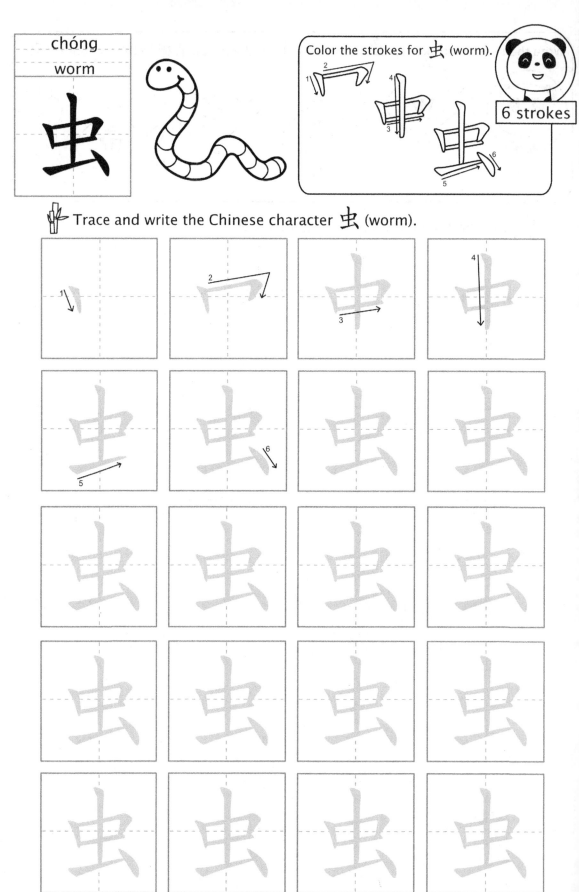

Color the strokes for 虫 (worm).

6 strokes

🎋 Trace and write the Chinese character 虫 (worm).

Write the missing stroke for 虫 on each worm from the panda 熊猫 to the bamboo 竹子.

熊猫
xióngmāo

竹子
zhúzi

Trace and write the Chinese character 虫.

zuò
sit

坐

Trace and write the Chinese character 坐 (sit).

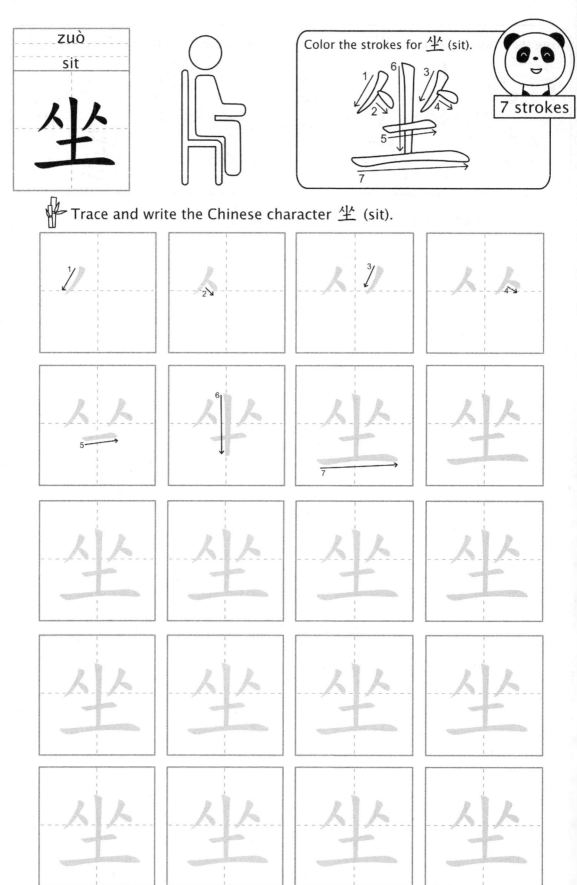

Write the missing stroke for 坐 in each circle from the panda 熊猫 to the bamboo 竹子.

熊猫
xióngmāo

竹子
zhúzi

Trace and write the Chinese character 坐 .

chē
car

车

Color the strokes for 车 (car).

4 strokes

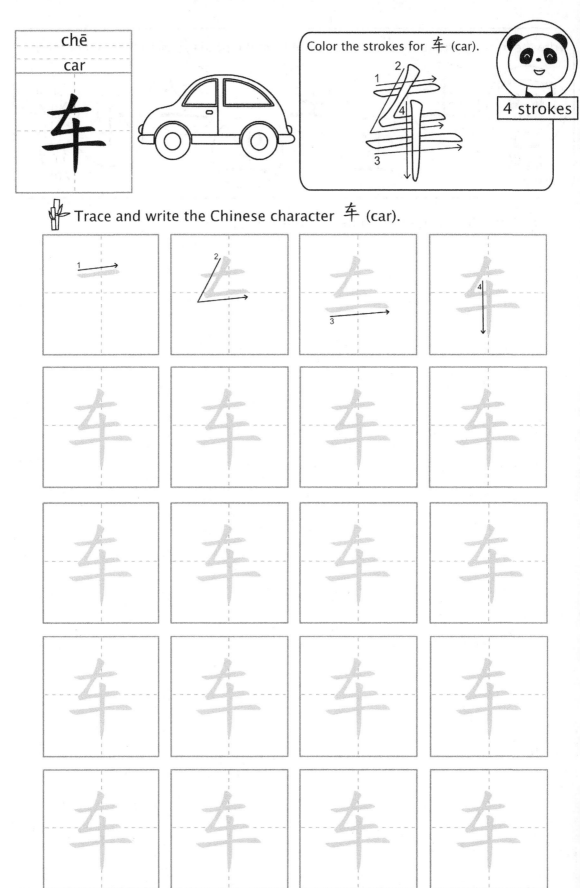

Trace and write the Chinese character 车 (car).

64

Write the missing stroke for 车 in each circle from the panda 熊猫 to the bamboo 竹子.

熊猫
xióngmāo

竹子
zhúzi

Trace and write the Chinese character 车.

Good Job!

Practice writing characters you have learned below.

Name

Date

Good Job!

Practice writing characters you have learned below.

67

mù
wood

木

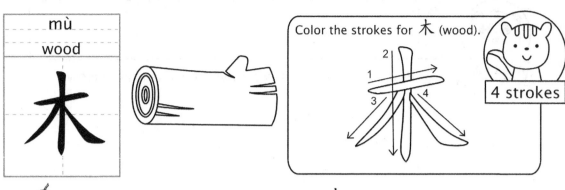

Color the strokes for 木 (wood).

4 strokes

🌰 Trace and write the Chinese character 木 (wood).

Write the missing stroke for 木 on each log from the squirrel 松鼠 to the acorn 橡子.

松鼠
sōngshǔ

木　　八　　大　　才

橡子
xiàng zi

Trace and write the Chinese character 木.

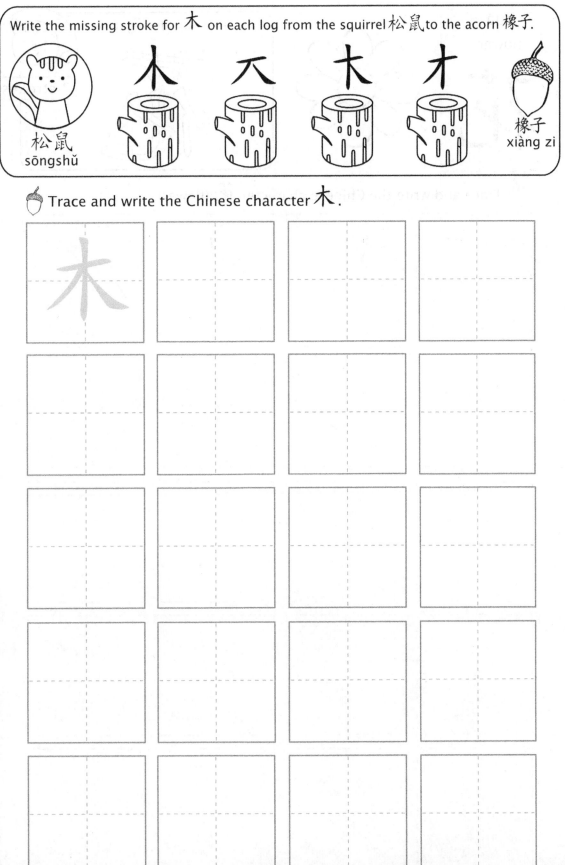

huā
flower

Color the strokes for 花 (flower).

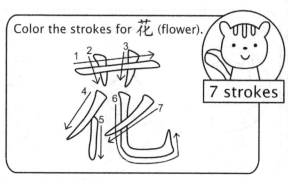

7 strokes

Trace and write the Chinese character 花 (flower).

70

Write the missing stroke for 花 on each flower from the squirrel 松鼠 to the acorn 橡子.

松鼠
sōngshǔ

橡子
xiàng zi

🌰 Trace and write the Chinese character 花.

shān
mountain

山

Color the strokes for 山 (mountain).

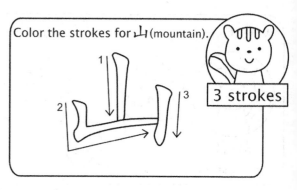

1
2
3

3 strokes

 Trace and write the Chinese character 山 (mountain).

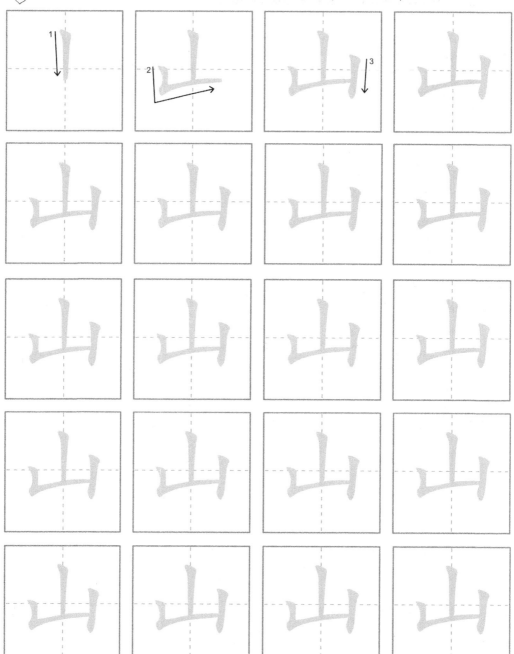

Write the missing stroke for 山 in each mountain from the squirrel 松鼠 to the acorn 橡子.

松鼠
sōngshǔ

橡子
xiàng zi

Trace and write the Chinese character 山.

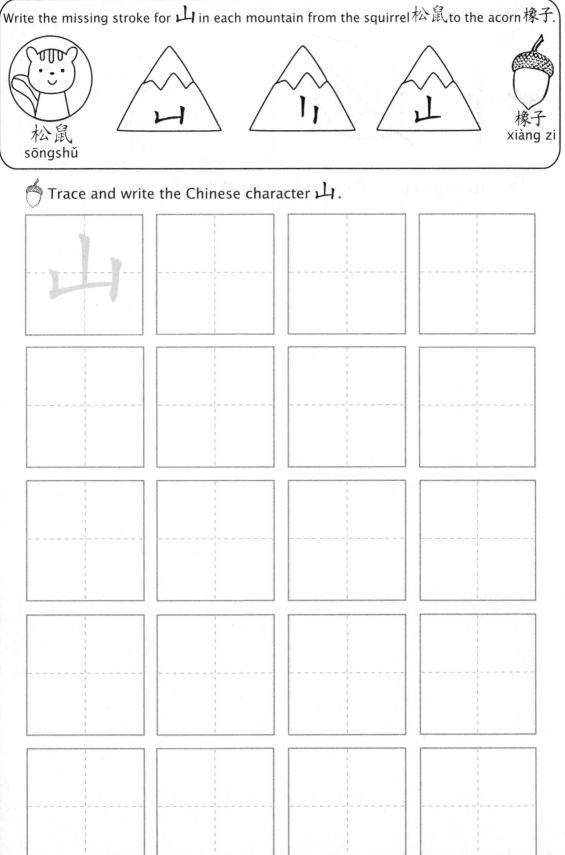

yè
leaf

叶

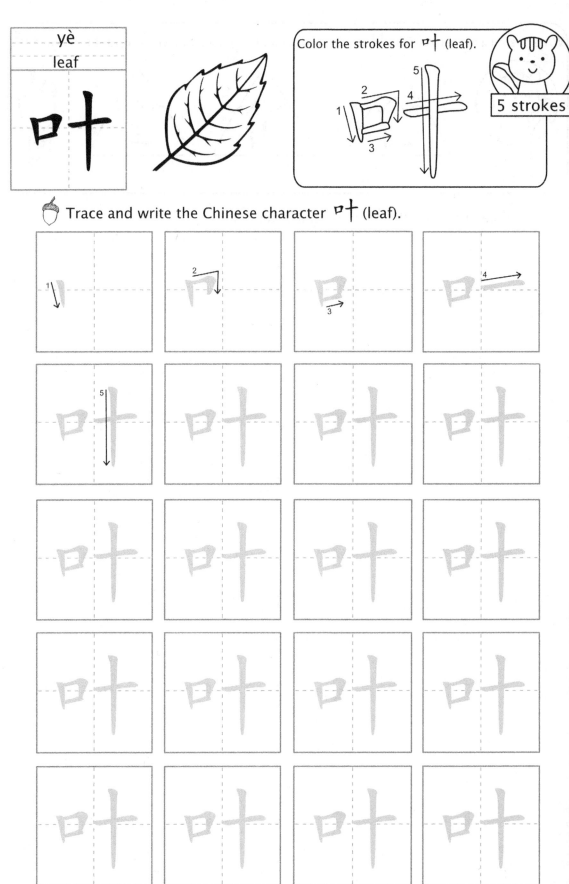

Color the strokes for 叶 (leaf).

5 strokes

Trace and write the Chinese character 叶 (leaf).

Write the missing stroke for 叶 on each leaf from the squirrel 松鼠 to the acorn 橡子.

松鼠
sōngshǔ

橡子
xiàng zi

Trace and write the Chinese character 叶.

| shuǐ |
| water |

水

Color the strokes for 水 (water).

4 strokes

🌰 Trace and write the Chinese character 水 (water).

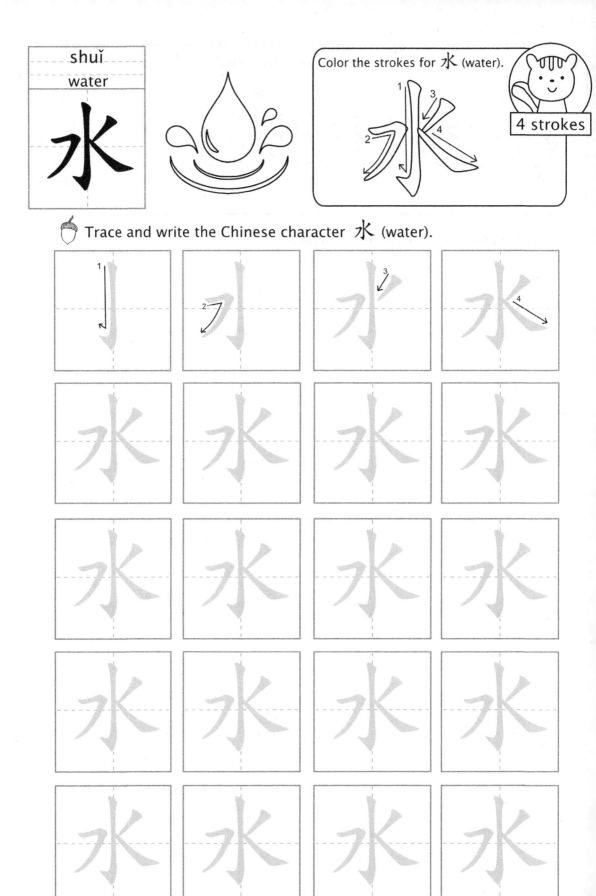

Write the missing stroke for 水 on each puddle from the squirrel 松鼠 to the acorn 橡子.

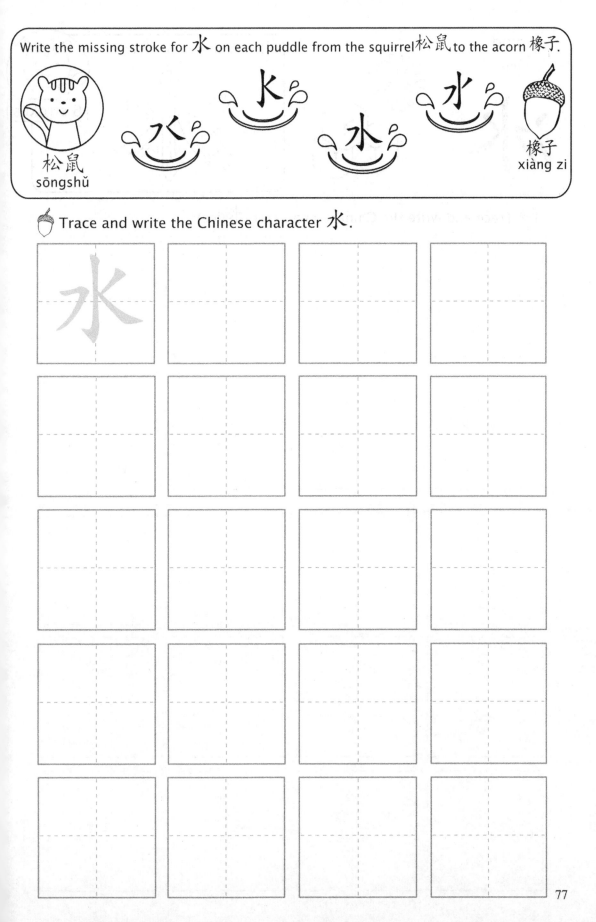

松鼠
sōngshǔ

橡子
xiàng zi

🌰 Trace and write the Chinese character 水.

bīng

ice

冰

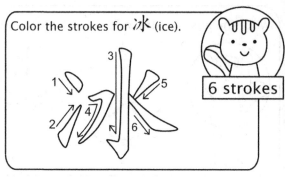

6 strokes

🌰 Trace and write the Chinese character 冰 (ice).

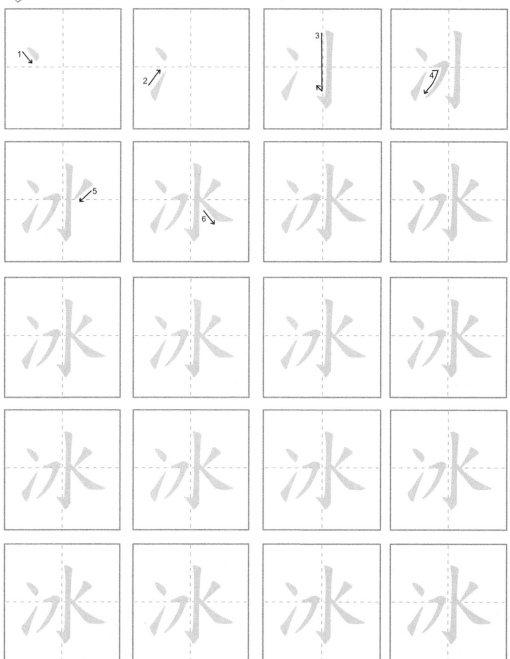

Write the missing stroke for 冰 on each ice cube from the squirrel 松鼠 to the acorn 橡子.

松鼠
sōngshǔ

橡子
xiàng zi

🌰 Trace and write the Chinese character 冰.

huǒ
fire

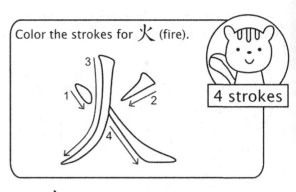

4 strokes

 Trace and write the Chinese character 火 (fire).

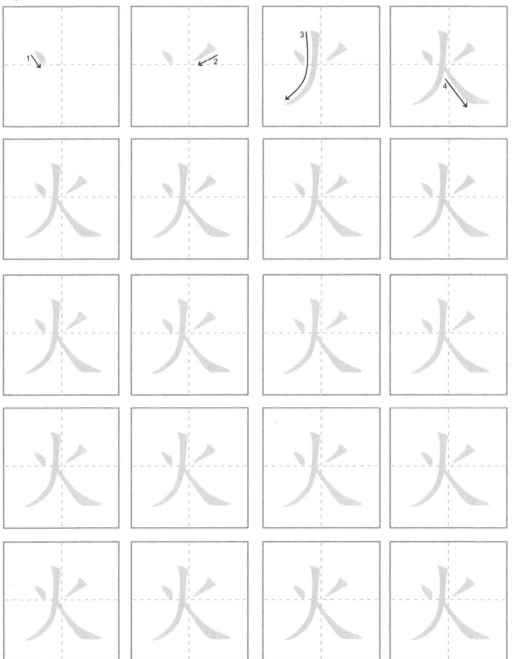

Write the missing stroke for 火 on the logs from the squirrel 松鼠 to the acorn 橡子.

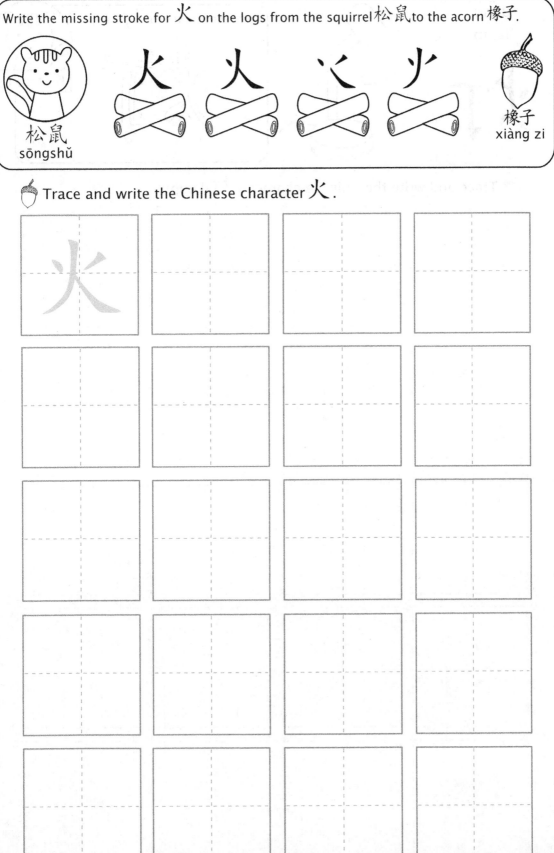

松鼠
sōngshǔ

橡子
xiàng zi

🌰 Trace and write the Chinese character 火.

dēng
lamp

灯

6 strokes

Trace and write the Chinese character 灯 (lamp).

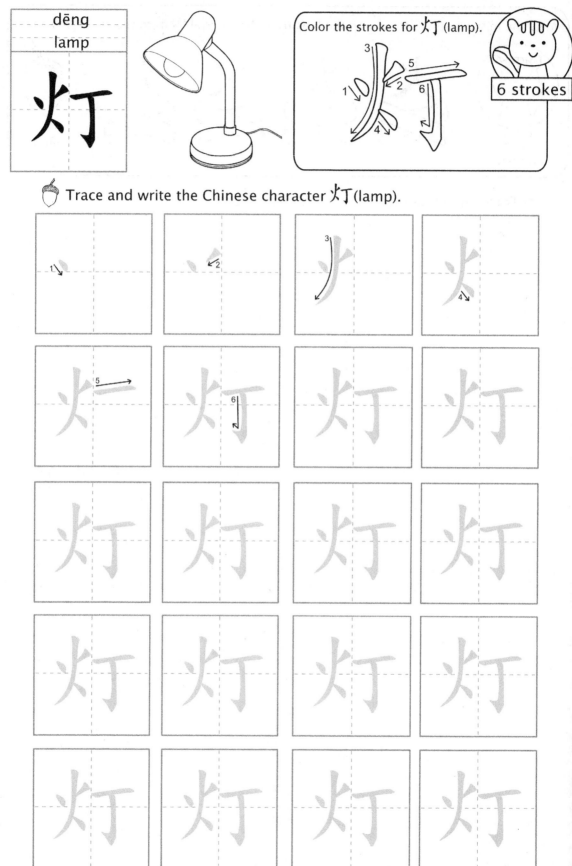

Write the missing stroke for 灯 in each light bulb from the squirrel 松鼠 to the acorn 橡子.

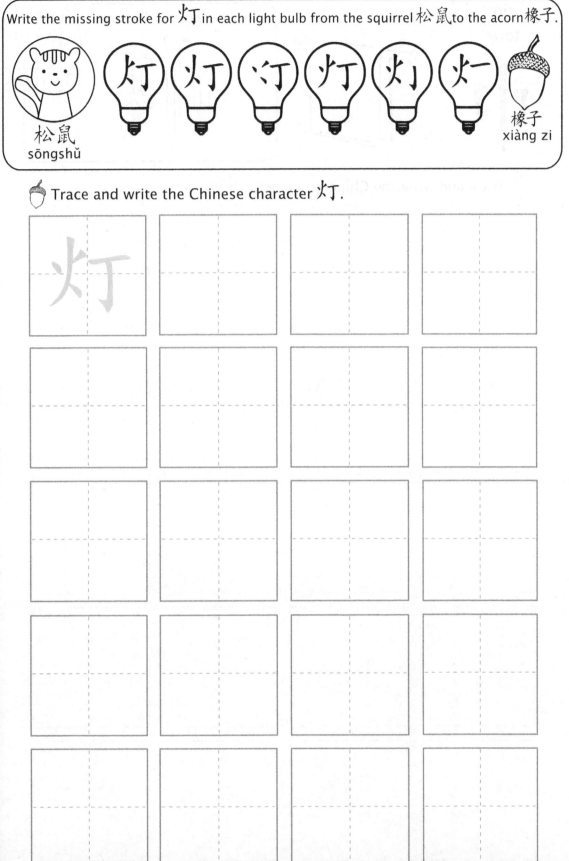

松鼠
sōngshǔ

橡子
xiàng zi

Trace and write the Chinese character 灯.

jīn

towel

巾

Color the strokes for 巾 (towel).

3 strokes

🌰 Trace and write the Chinese character 巾 (towel).

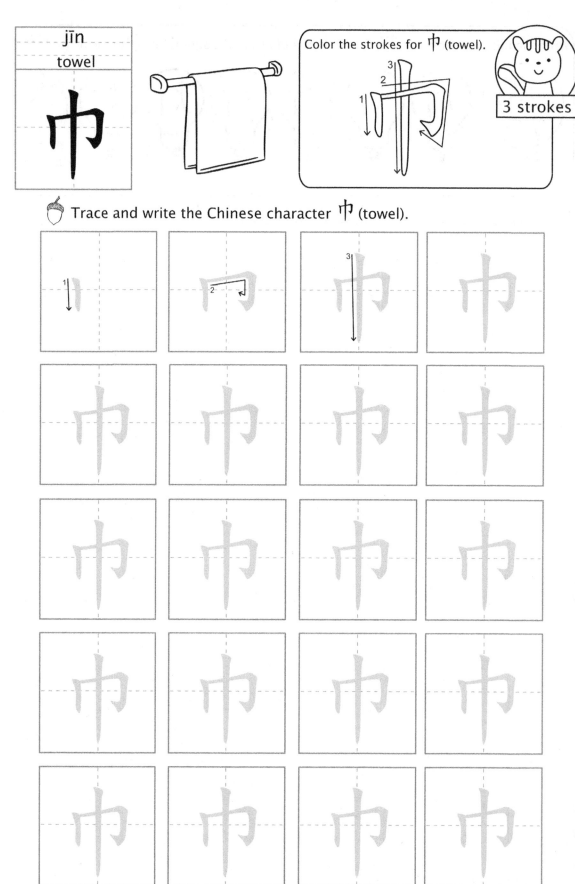

Write the missing stroke for 巾 on each towel from the squirrel 松鼠 to the acorn 橡子.

松鼠
sōngshǔ

巾 丨 冂 巾 丨 冂

橡子
xiàng zi

Trace and write the Chinese character 巾.

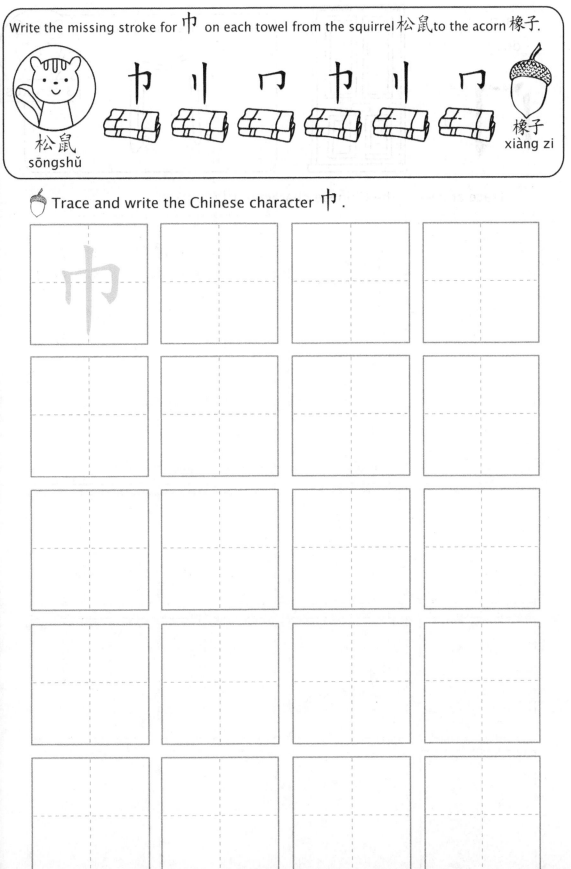

mén
door

门

Color the strokes for 门 (door).

1
2
3

3 strokes

🌰 Trace and write the Chinese character 门 (door).

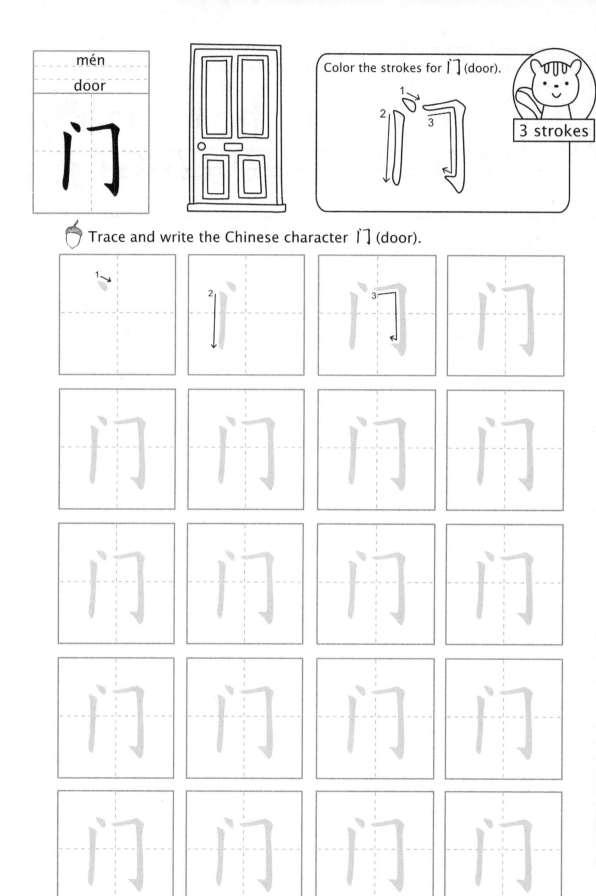

Write the missing stroke for 门 on each house from the squirrel 松鼠 to the acorn 橡子.

松鼠
sōngshǔ

橡子
xiàng zi

Trace and write the Chinese character 门.

Good Job!

Practice writing characters you have learned below.

Name

Date

Practice writing characters you have learned below.

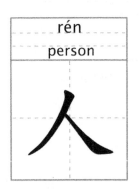

rén

person

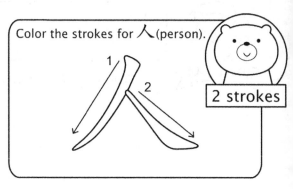

Color the strokes for 人 (person).

2 strokes

Trace and write the Chinese character 人 (person).

Write the missing stroke for 人 on the person from the bear 熊 to the honey 蜜糖.

熊
xióng

蜜糖
mì táng

Trace and write the Chinese character 人.

yǒu
friend

友

Color the strokes for 友 (friend).

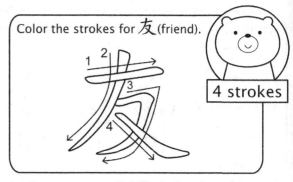

4 strokes

🐝 Trace and write the Chinese character 友 (friend).

Write the missing stroke for 友 on the friends from the bear 熊 to the honey 蜜糖.

熊
xióng

友　又　大　方

蜜糖
mì táng

Trace and write the Chinese character 友.

友

shǒu
hand

手

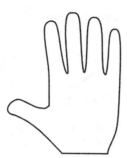

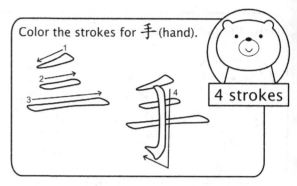

Color the strokes for 手 (hand).

4 strokes

🐝 Trace and write the Chinese character 手 (hand).

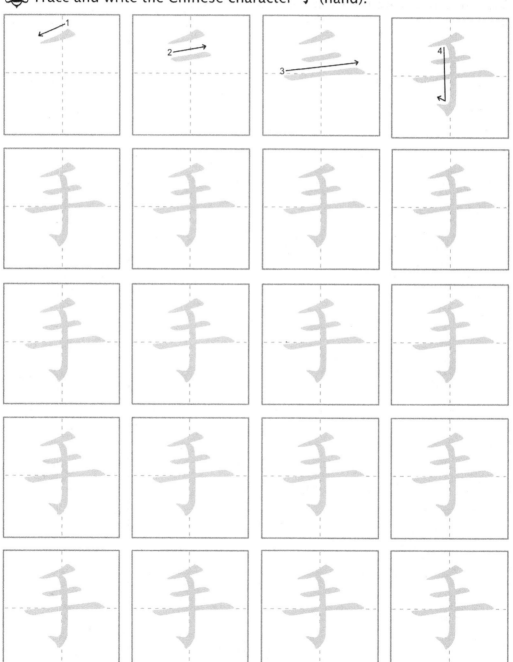

Write the missing stroke for 手 on each hand from the bear 熊 to the honey 蜜糖.

熊
xióng

蜜糖
mì táng

Trace and write the Chinese character 手.

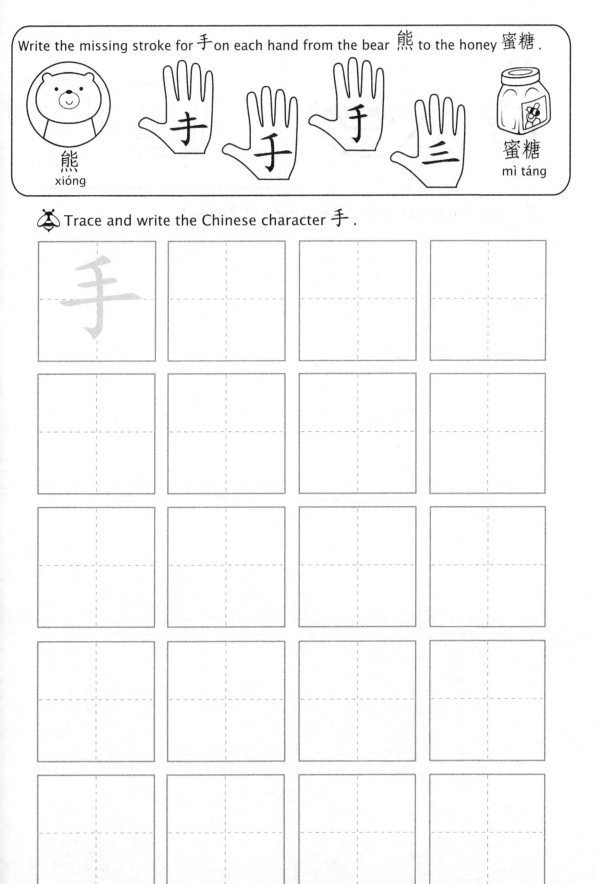

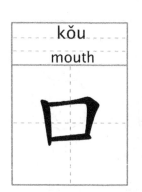

kǒu

mouth

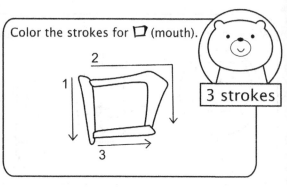

2

1

3

3 strokes

Trace and write the Chinese character 口 (mouth).

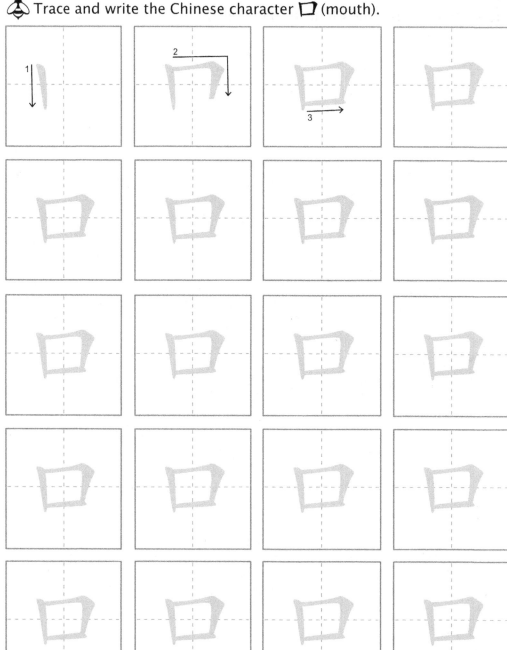

Write the missing stroke for 口 in each mouth from the bear 熊 to the honey 蜜糖 .

熊
xióng

蜜糖
mì táng

Trace and write the Chinese character 口 .

yá

tooth

牙

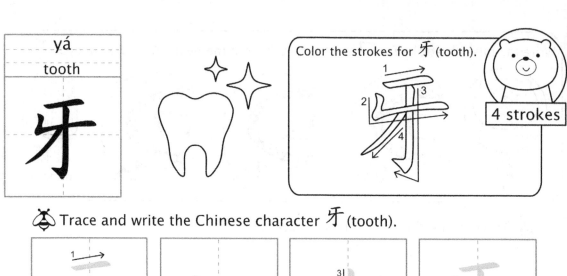

Color the strokes for 牙 (tooth).

4 strokes

🐝 Trace and write the Chinese character 牙 (tooth).

Write the missing stroke for 牙 on each tooth from the bear 熊 to the honey 蜜糖 .

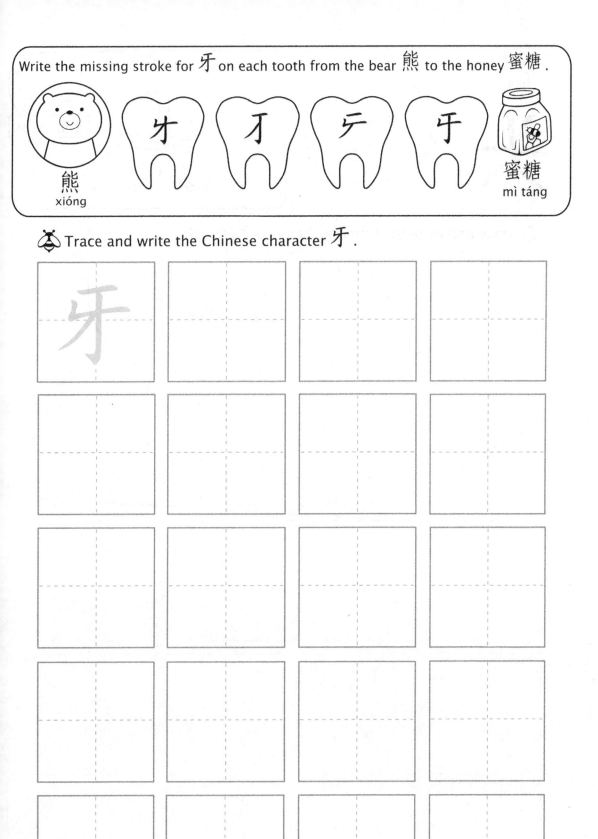

熊
xióng

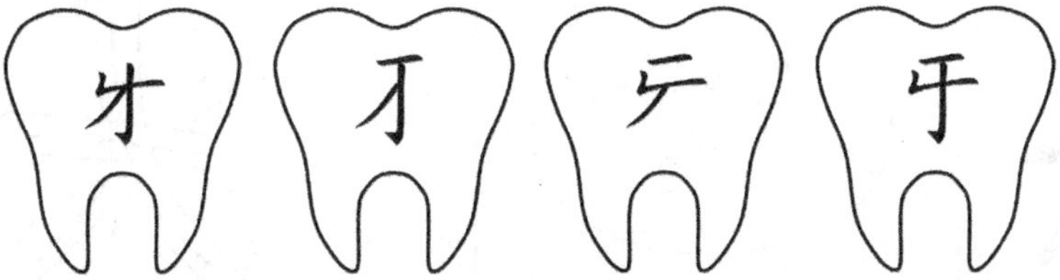

蜜糖
mì táng

Trace and write the Chinese character 牙 .

tóu
head

头

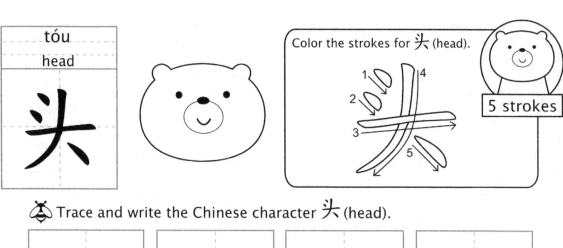

Color the strokes for 头 (head).

5 strokes

🐝 Trace and write the Chinese character 头 (head).

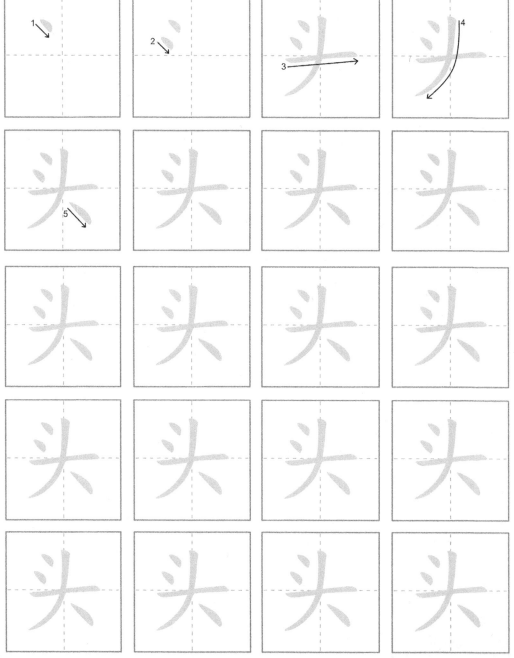

Write the missing stroke for 头 in each head from the bear 熊 to the honey 蜜糖 .

熊
xióng

头   头   头

头   六

蜜糖
mì táng

Trace and write the Chinese character 头 .

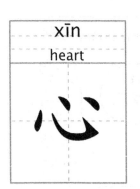

xīn

heart

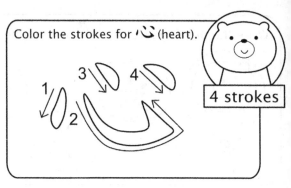

Color the strokes for 心 (heart).

4 strokes

🐝 Trace and write the Chinese character 心 (heart).

102

Write the missing stroke for 心 in each heart from the bear 熊 to the honey 蜜糖.

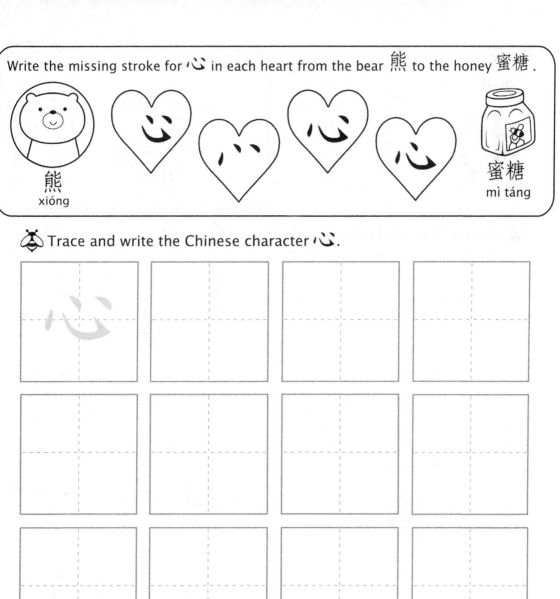

熊
xióng

蜜糖
mì táng

Trace and write the Chinese character 心.

shū
book

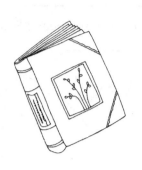

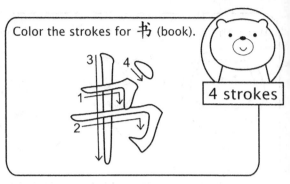

4 strokes

Trace and write the Chinese character 书 (book).

Write the missing stroke for 书 on the books from the bear 熊 to the honey 蜜糖 .

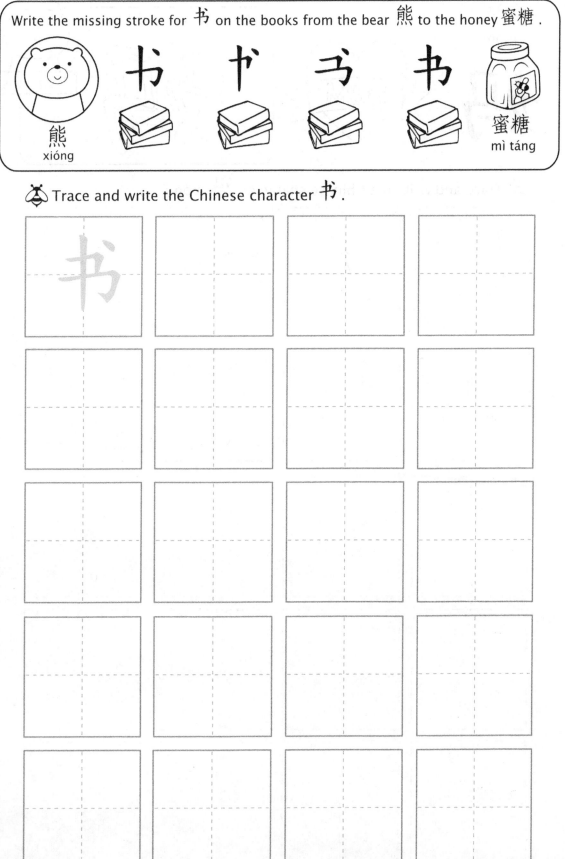

熊
xióng

蜜糖
mì táng

Trace and write the Chinese character 书 .

mā
mom

妈

MOM

Color the strokes for 妈 (mom).

6 strokes

Trace and write the Chinese character 妈 (mom).

Write the missing stroke for 妈 in the hearts from the bear 熊 to the honey 蜜糖.

熊
xióng

冯
圬
妈
妈
奵
妈

蜜糖
mì táng

🐝 Trace and write the Chinese character 妈.

妈

| bà |
| dad |

爸

Color the strokes for 爸 (dad).

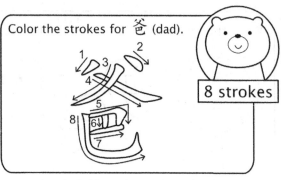

8 strokes

Trace and write the Chinese character 爸 (dad).

Write the missing stroke for 爸 in the medals from the bear 熊 to the honey 蜜糖.

熊
xióng

蜜糖
mì táng

🐝 Trace and write the Chinese character 爸.

Good Job!

Practice writing characters you have learned below.

Good Job!

Practice writing characters you have learned below.

Made in United States
North Haven, CT
22 November 2024

60773361R00063